W9-AVC-791

P
PRESCHOOL
AGES 3–5

Letters
Learning Fun Workbook

For information about permission to reproduce selections from this book for
an entire school or school district, please contact permissions@highlights.com.

Published by Highlights Learning • 815 Church Street • Honesdale, Pennsylvania 18431
ISBN: 978-1-68437-279-9
Mfg. 08/2019
Printed in Guangzhou, Guangdong, China
First edition
10 9 8 7 6 5 4 3 2

For assistance in the preparation of this book, the editors would like to thank:
Vanessa Maldonado, MSEd; MS Literacy Ed. K–12; Reading/LA Consultant Cert.; K–5 Literacy Instructional Coach
Kristin Ward, MS Curriculum, Instruction, and Assessment; K–5 Mathematics Instructional Coach
Jump Start Press, Inc.

A

This is an uppercase A.

a

This is a lowercase a.

What are the ants having for dinner?

Trace the letters. Then write your own.

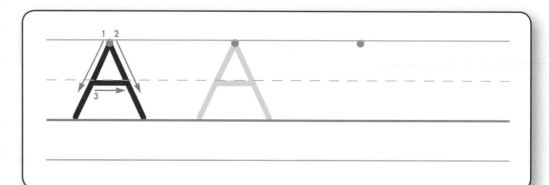

A is for Ant. Follow the A's to help Antonio get home in time for dinner.

B
b

This is an **uppercase** B.

This is a **lowercase** b.

Trace the letters. Then write your own.

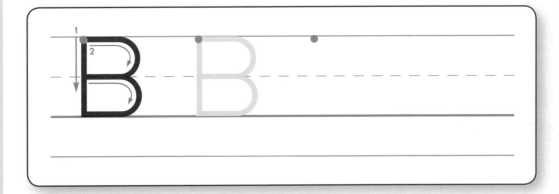

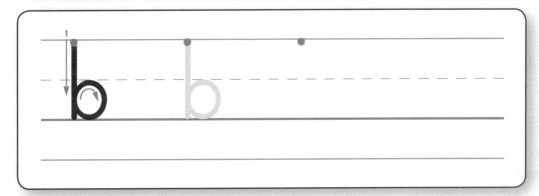

B is for Birthday. It's Becky's birthday! Put the pictures in order. Use **1, 2,** and **3** to show what happened first, second, and third.

Use the pictures to tell a story about this party.

C

This is an
uppercase C.

c

This is a
lowercase c.

Say this
tongue twister
3 times:
*Cats crawl
and claw.*

Trace the letters. Then write your own.

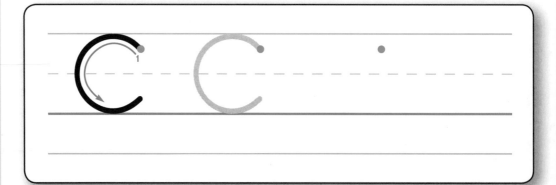

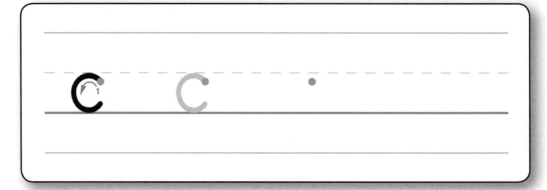

C is for Cat. Draw an X to cross out the cat in each row that does not match the others.

D

This is an uppercase D.

This is a lowercase d.

What is your favorite dinosaur?

Trace the letters. Then write your own.

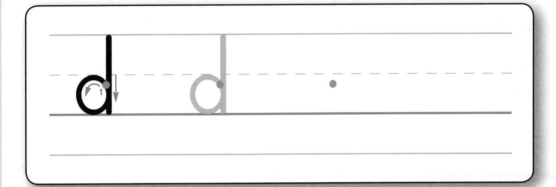

D is for Dinosaur. Color in each shape that has a **D** with a green crayon. Color in each shape that has a **d** with a brown crayon.

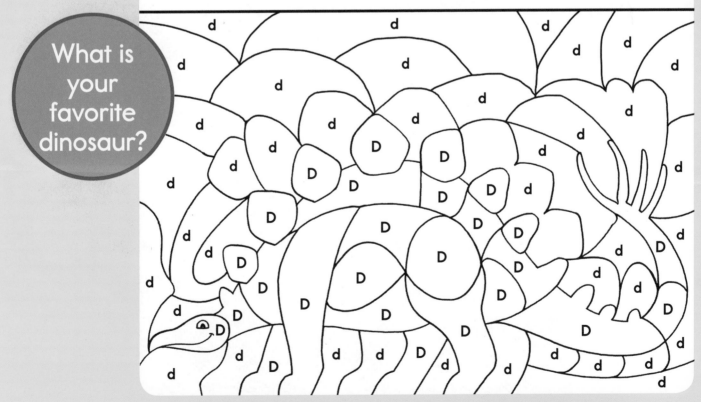

E

This is an
uppercase E.

e

This is a
lowercase e.

Trace the letters. Then write your own.

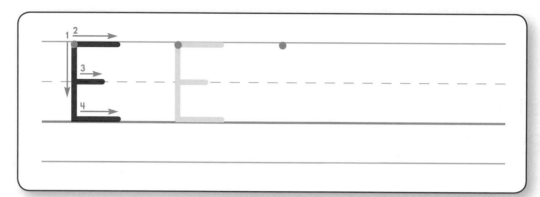

E is for Elephant. How many E's can you find hidden in the picture?

Can you think of another animal that begins with the letter E?

F

This is an uppercase F.

f

This is a lowercase f.

Trace the letters. Then write your own.

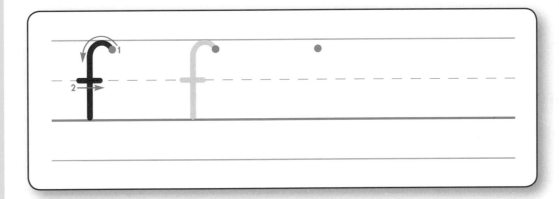

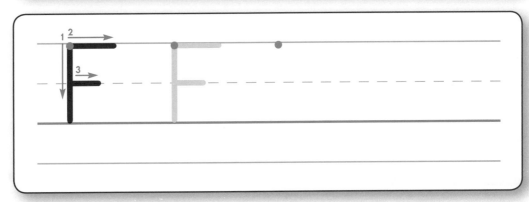

F is for Flag. Draw a line from each flag to its match.

Can you think of 5 other words that begin with the letter F?

G

This is an uppercase G.

g

This is a lowercase g.

Trace the letters. Then write your own.

G is for Gecko. Which gecko has the most spots on its back? Which gecko has the fewest spots?

Say this tongue twister 3 times: *Geckos get going.*

H

This is an uppercase H.

h

This is a lowercase h.

Trace the letters. Then write your own.

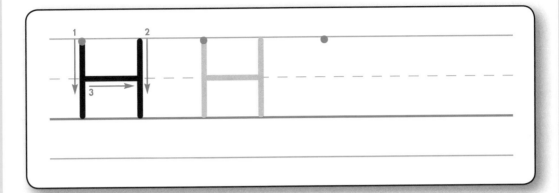

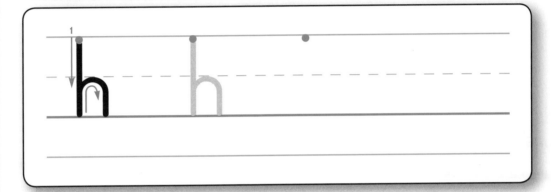

H is for Hat. Everyone's hat has blown off! Draw a line from each hat to its owner.

How many H's can you find hidden in the picture?

I

This is an uppercase I.

This is a lowercase i.

What do you like to do in winter?

Trace the letters. Then write your own.

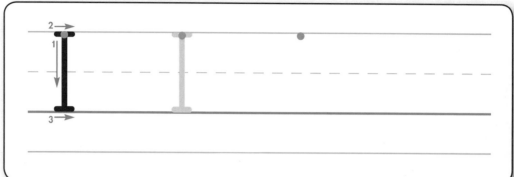

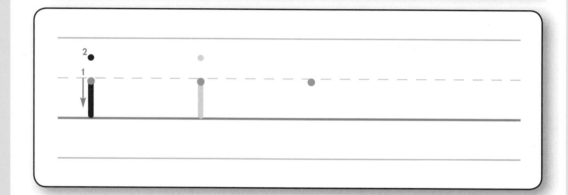

I is for Ice Skate. Follow the I's to help Issa reach her dad.

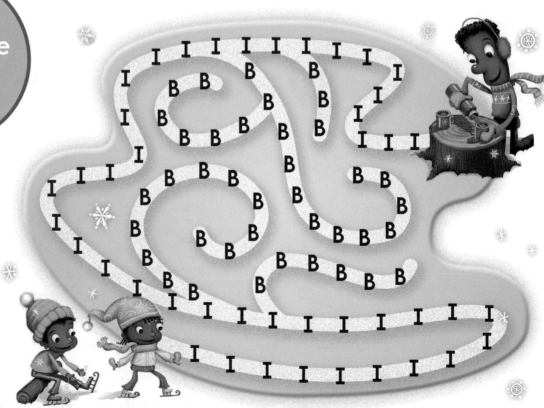

J

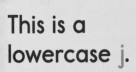

This is an uppercase J.

This is a lowercase j.

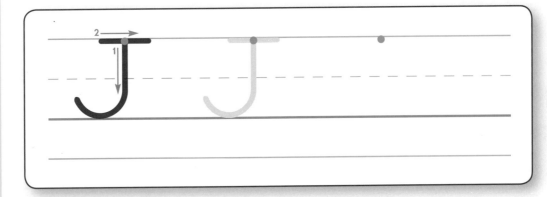

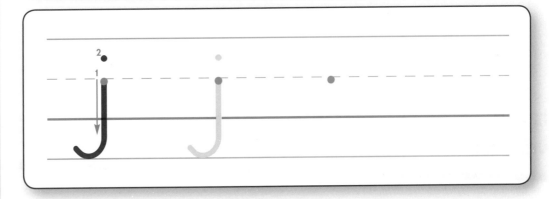

J is for Juggle. Draw a line from each juggling pin to its match.

Say this tongue twister 3 times: *Jared juggled joyfully.*

K

This is an uppercase K.

k

This is a lowercase k.

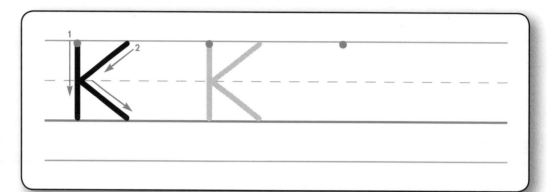

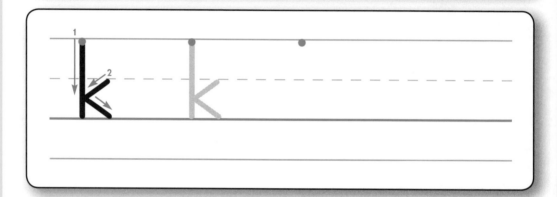

K is for Kite. Use crayons or markers to decorate this kite.

Have you ever flown a kite?

L

This is an uppercase L.

This is a lowercase l.

Trace the letters. Then write your own.

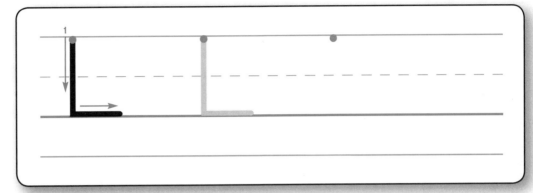

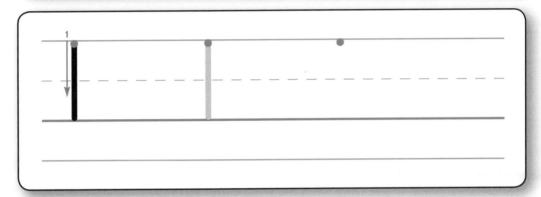

L is for Ladybug. How many L's can you find hidden in the picture?

Can you find 5 ladybugs?

M

This is an uppercase M.

m

This is a lowercase m.

Trace the letters. Then write your own.

M is for Music. Connect the dots from **A** to **M** to see what this man is playing to make music.

N

This is an uppercase N.

n

This is a lowercase n.

Trace the letters. Then write your own.

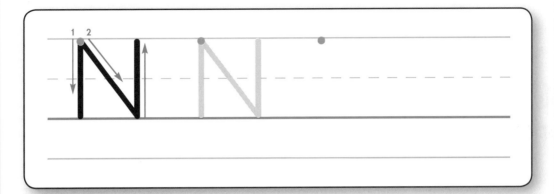

N is for Nest. Follow the N's to help the bird get to her nest.

Can you name 2 kinds of birds?

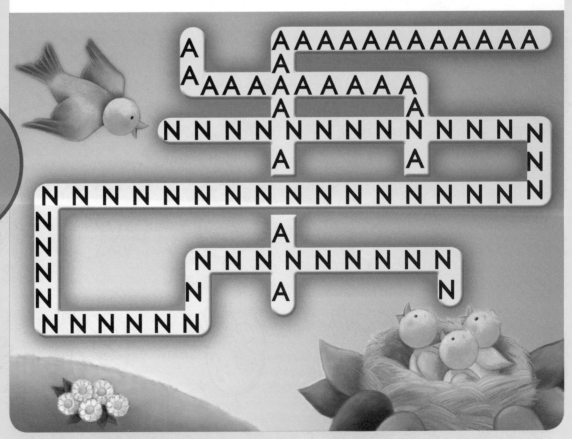

This is an uppercase O.

This is a lowercase o.

Trace the letters. Then write your own.

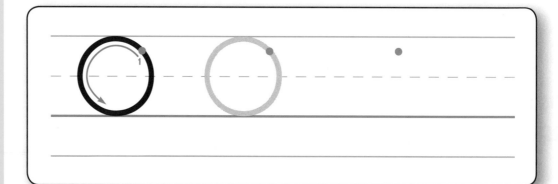

O is for Owl. Draw an **X** to cross out the owl in each row that does not match the others.

What other animals begin with the letter O?

P

This is an uppercase P.

p

This is a lowercase p.

Give the puppy a name that begins with the letter P.

Trace the letters. Then write your own.

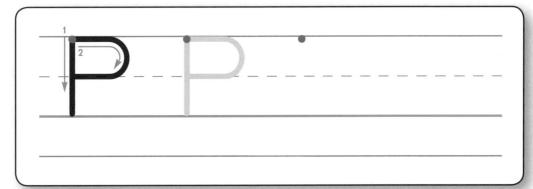

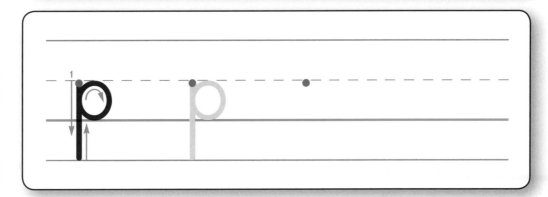

P is for Puppy. Put the pictures in order. Use **1**, **2**, and **3** to show what happened first, second, and third.

Q

This is an uppercase Q.

q

This is a lowercase q.

Trace the letters. Then write your own.

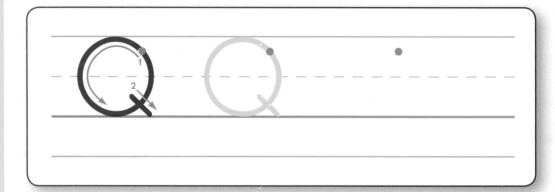

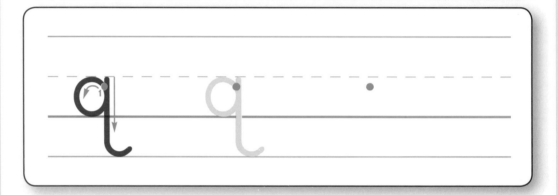

Q is for Quarter. Circle the quarters. How many did you find?

1 quarter = 25 cents.

R

This is an
uppercase R.

r

This is a
lowercase r.

Trace the letters. Then write your own.

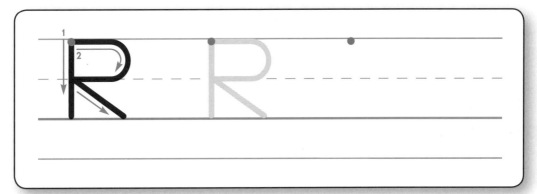

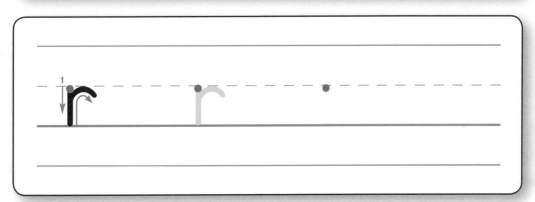

R is for Robot. Draw some legs on the red robot. Draw a head on the yellow robot.

Say this tongue twister 3 times: *Robots rolled red wagons.*

S

This is an uppercase S.

s

This is a lowercase s.

Trace the letters. Then write your own.

S S S

s s

S is for Shoe. Help Sam find the one pair of shoes that is an exact match.

Can you name a type of shoe that starts with the letter S?

T

This is an uppercase T.

t

This is a lowercase t.

Trace the letters. Then write your own.

T is for Tugboat. Color in each shape that has a T with a red crayon. Color in each shape that has a t with a black crayon.

A tugboat can push or pull heavy loads. Can you think of another type of vehicle that begins with the letter T?

U

This is an uppercase U.

u

This is a lowercase u.

Trace the letters. Then write your own.

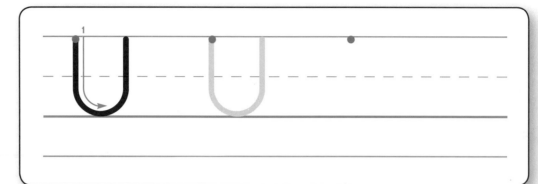

U is for Unicycle. Uma wants to ride her unicycle. Follow the U's to get Uma to her unicycle.

Would you like to ride a unicycle? Why or why not?

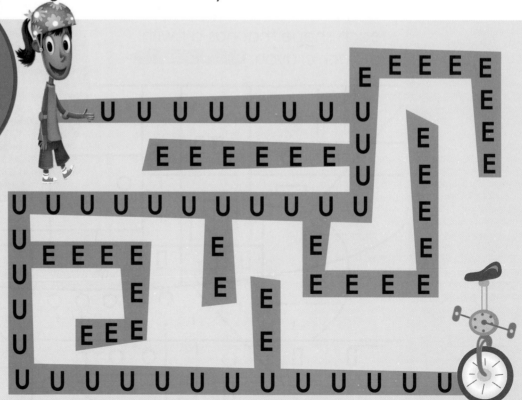

V

This is an uppercase V.

v

This is a lowercase v.

Trace the letters. Then write your own.

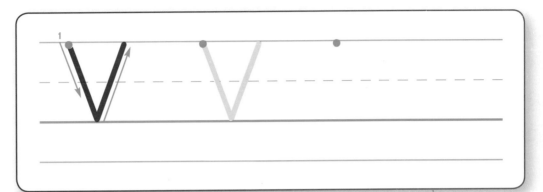

Can you name some of the vegetables on this page?

V is for Vegetable. Draw an **X** to cross out the vegetable in each row that does not match the others.

This is an
uppercase W.

This is a
lowercase w.

Trace the letters. Then write your own.

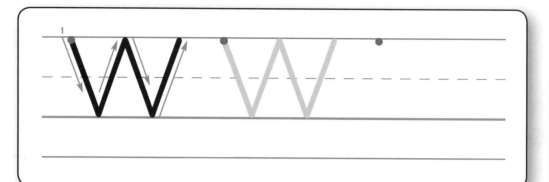

W is for Watermelon. Find the **2** watermelon slices that match.

Which slice has the most black seeds? Which slice has the most white seeds?

This is an uppercase X.

This is a lowercase x.

Say this tongue twister 3 times: *One box, three foxes*

Trace the letters. Then write your own.

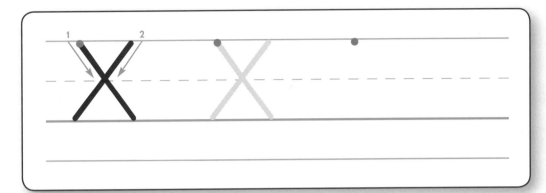

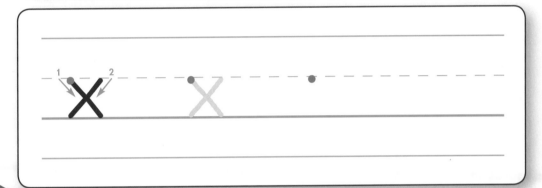

X is for X-ray. Can you find **3** differences between these X-rays?

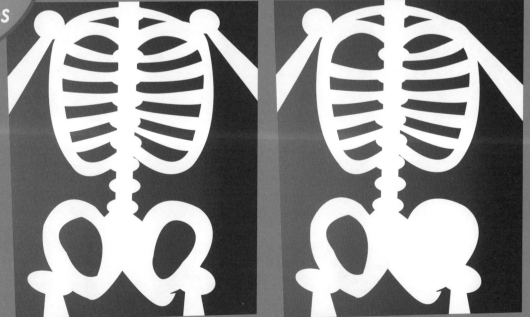

Y
y

This is an uppercase Y.

This is a lowercase y.

Trace the letters. Then write your own.

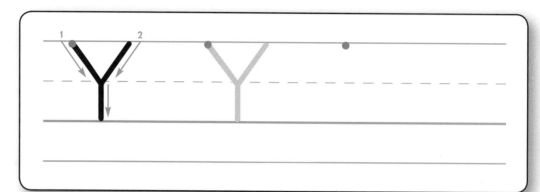

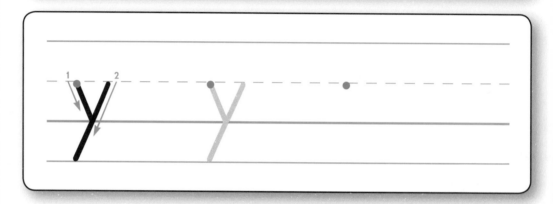

Y is for Yarn. Can you find **5** Y's hidden in the picture?

How many yellow balls of yarn can you find?

Z

This is an uppercase Z.

z

This is a lowercase z.

Trace the letters. Then write your own.

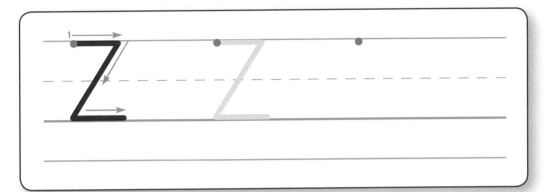

What can you find on a coat that begins with the letter Z and rhymes with the word *flipper*?

Z is for Zebra. What is the zebra trying on? Connect the dots from N to Z to find out.

Trace the Alphabet

Trace all the uppercase letters of the alphabet.

A B C D E F

G H I J K L M

N O P Q R S

T U V W X Y Z

Emergent Literacy: Uppercase Letters

Trace the Alphabet

Trace all the lowercase letters of the alphabet.

a b c d e f

g h i j k l m

n o p q r s

t u v w x y z

Letter Match-Up

Match the uppercase letter to the lowercase letter.

 A ○

○ b

 B ○

○ d

 C ○

○ g

 D ○

○ f

 E ○

○ a

 F ○

○ c

 G ○

○ e

Emergent Literacy: Uppercase and Lowercase Letters

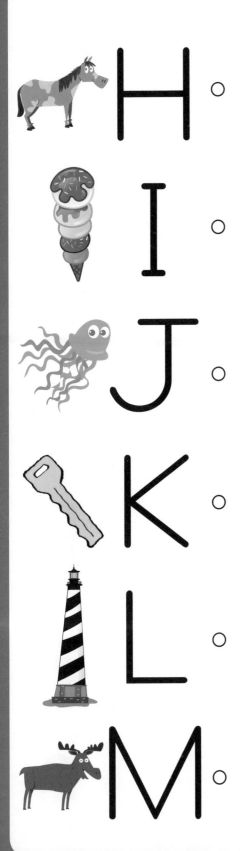

H

I

J

K

L

M

m

j

l

i

k

h

Letter Match-Up

Match the uppercase letter to the lowercase letter.

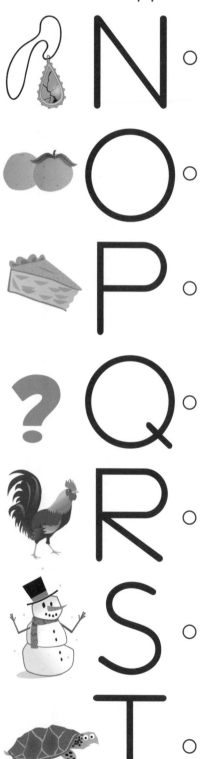

N ○

O ○

P ○

Q ○

R ○

S ○

T ○

○ q

○ r

○ o

○ s

○ p

○ t

○ n

Emergent Literacy: Uppercase and Lowercase Letters

 U ○   ○ W

V ○   ○ z

 W ○   ○ x

X ○   ○ u

Y ○   ○ v

Z ○   ○ y

Uppercase & Lowercase

Trace the uppercase letter. Then write the lowercase letter that matches.

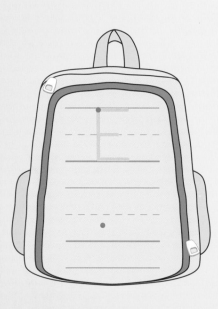

Emergent Writing: Uppercase and Lowercase Letters

Uppercase & Lowercase

Trace the uppercase letter. Then write the lowercase letter that matches.

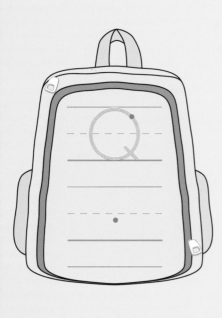

Lowercase & Uppercase

Trace the lowercase letter. Then write the uppercase letter that matches.

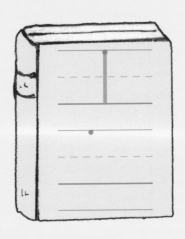

Lowercase & Uppercase

Trace the lowercase letter. Then write the uppercase letter that matches.

ABC Order

Connect the dots from **A** to **Z** to find something you can make at the beach.

abc Order

Connect the dots from **a** to **z** to find an animal that likes ice and snow.

ABC Order

Hera the hermit crab is looking for a new shell. She can move only in alphabetical order. Write the missing uppercase letters to help her find the perfect shell.

A ☐ C D ☐

J ☐ H G F

K ☐ M N ☐ P

☐ T S ☐ Q

V W ☐ Y Z

abc Order

Pick your way through the pumpkin patch.
Write the missing lowercase letters in
alphabetical order.

P PRESCHOOL

Congratulations!

_____
(your name)

**worked hard
and finished the**

Letters

Learning Fun Workbook

Answers

Page 2
Aa

Page 3
Bb

Page 4
Cc

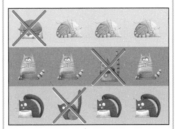

Page 5
Dd

Page 6
Ee

There are 6 **E**'s.

Page 7
Ff

Page 8
Gg

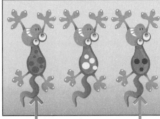

Most spots   Fewest spots

Page 9
Hh

There are 5 **H**'s.

Page 10
Ii

Page 11
Jj

Page 13
Ll

There are 7 **L**'s.

Page 14
Mm

It's a trumpet.

Page 15
Nn

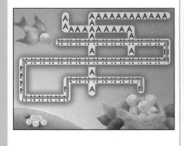

Page 16
Oo

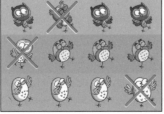

Page 17
Pp

Page 18
Qq

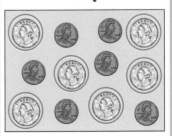

There are 6 quarters.

Answers

Page 20
S s

SNEAKER or SANDAL
You may have thought
of others.

Page 21
T t

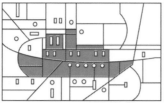
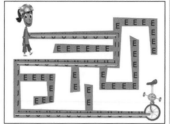

TRUCK or TRICYCLE
You may have thought
of others.

Page 22
U u

Page 23
V v

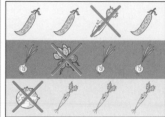

Peas, celery, onions, beets,
lettuce, and carrots

Page 24
W w

Most white seeds

Most black seeds

Page 25
X x

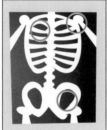

Page 26
Y y

There are 5 yellow balls
of yarn.

Page 27
Z z

It's a tie.
A *zipper* can be found
on a coat.

Page 42
ABC Order

It's a sand castle.

Page 43
abc Order

It's a polar bear.

Page 44
ABC Order

Page 45
abc Order

Inside Back Cover
Scavenger Hunt

1. Page 4
2. Page 24
3. Page 16
4. Page 6
5. Page 27
6. Page 22